Copyright

This license is for personal use only. This workbook is for personal use or use as a gift for someone. However, reselling, or any commercial use of this product is not allowed.

This handwriting practice book list step by step directions for you to help your child form letters. Sing/Chant the directions as your child writes the letters for reinforcement.

Additionally each picture can be coloured.

1. Up the hill.
2. Down the hill.
3. Across the river.

 1. Around the world.
2. Down the hill.

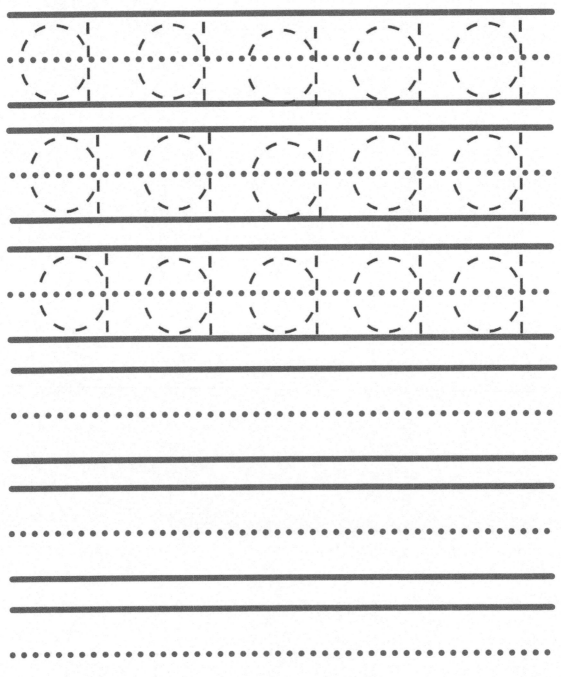

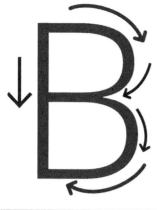

1. Down the hill.
2. Half the way on top.
3. Half the way on the bottom.

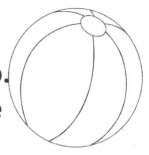

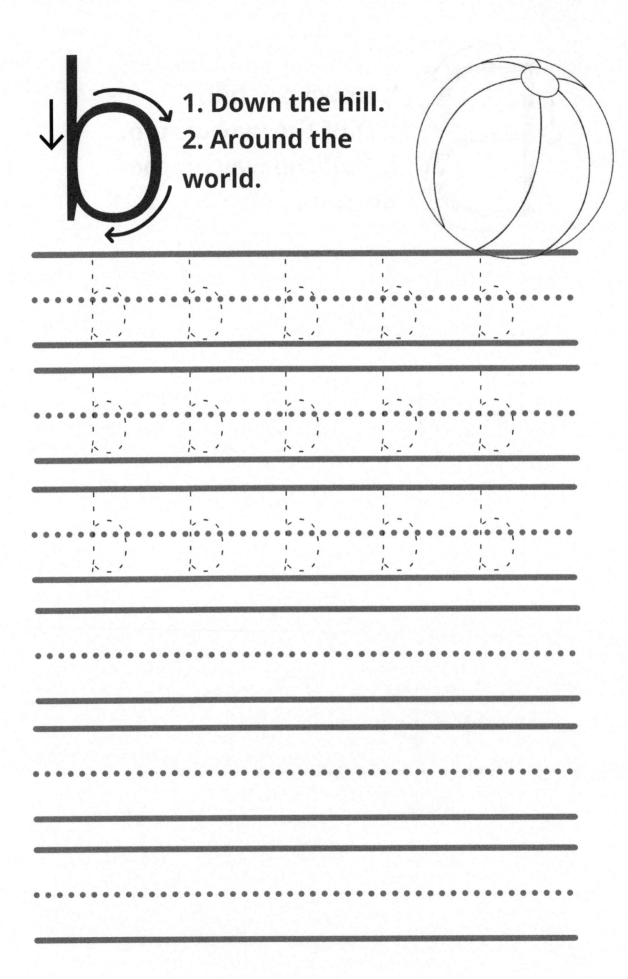

1. Bring it around town.

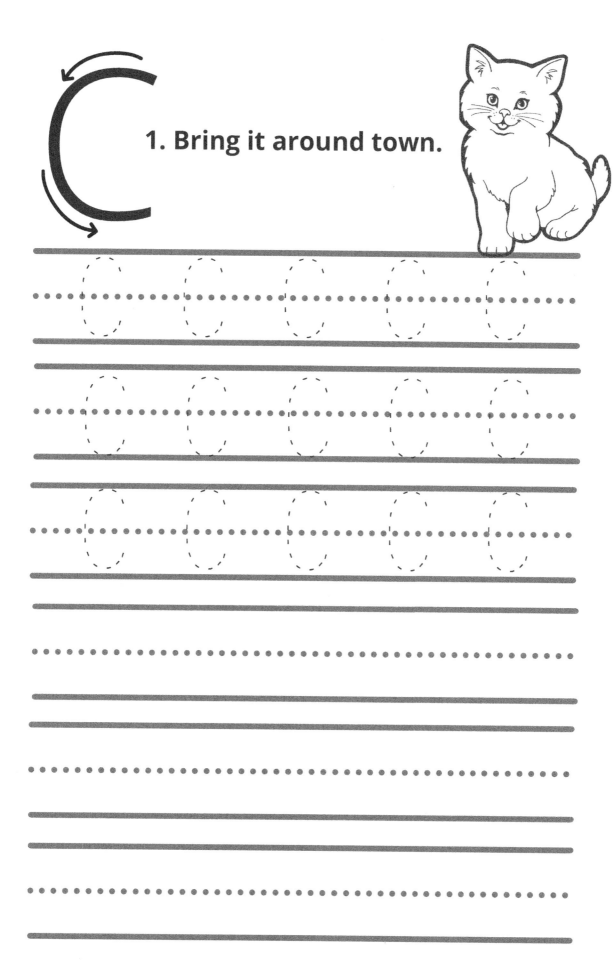

1. Bring it around town.

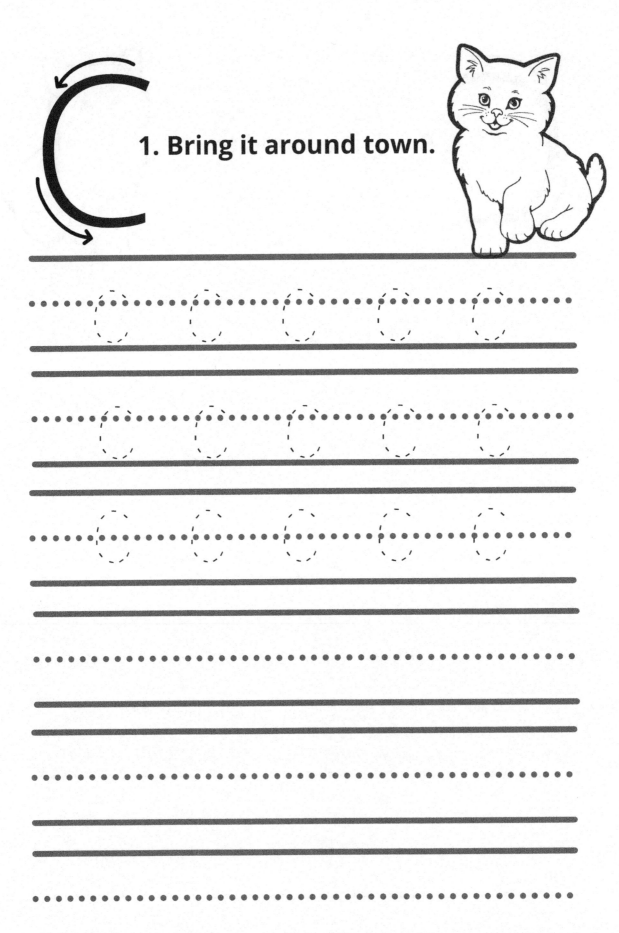

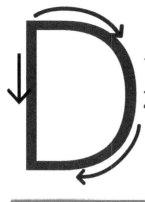

1. Down the hill.
2. Around the world.

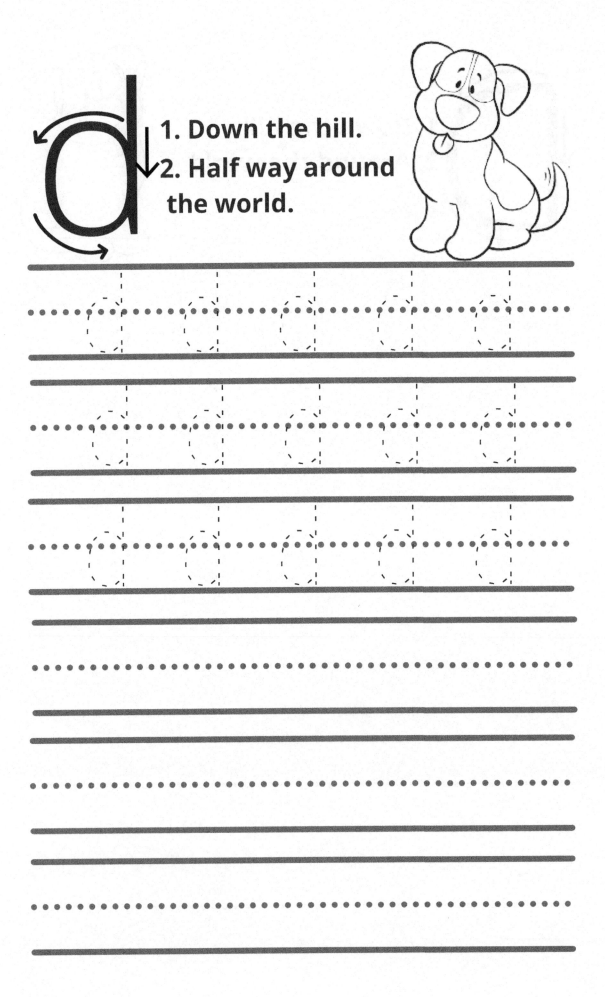

1. Down the hill.
2. To the elephant.
3. To the elephant.
4. To the elephant.

1. To the elephant.
2. Bring it around town.

1. Down the hill.
2. To the frog.
3. To the frog.

1. Off the cliff.
2. To the frog.

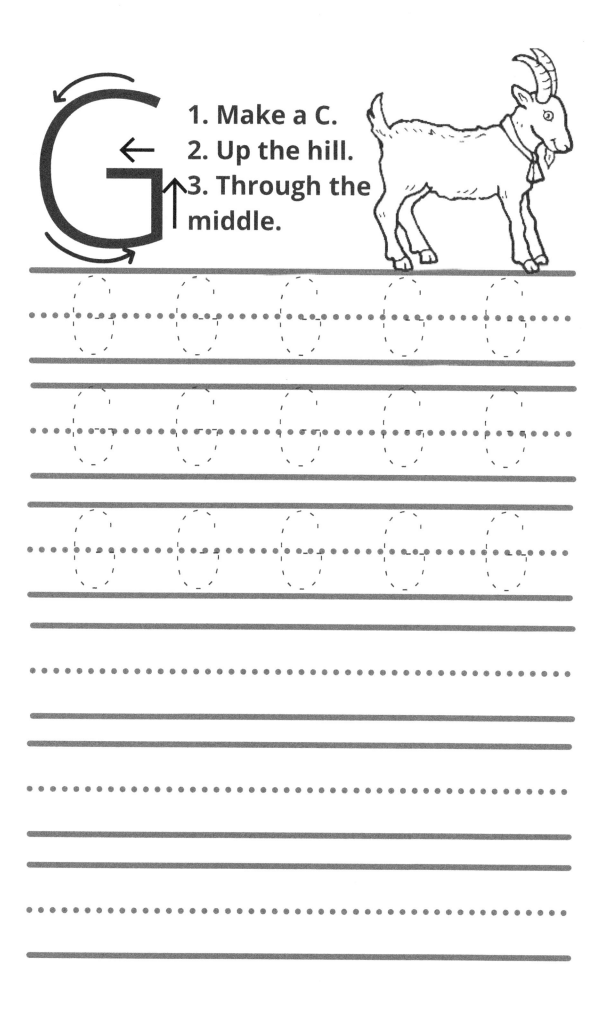

1. Make a C.
2. Up the hill.
3. Through the middle.

1. Down the cliff in the lake.
2. Half way around the world.

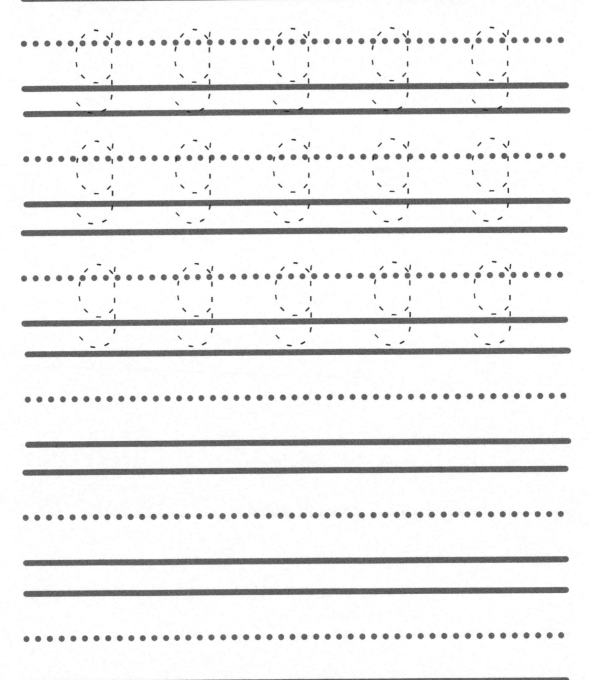

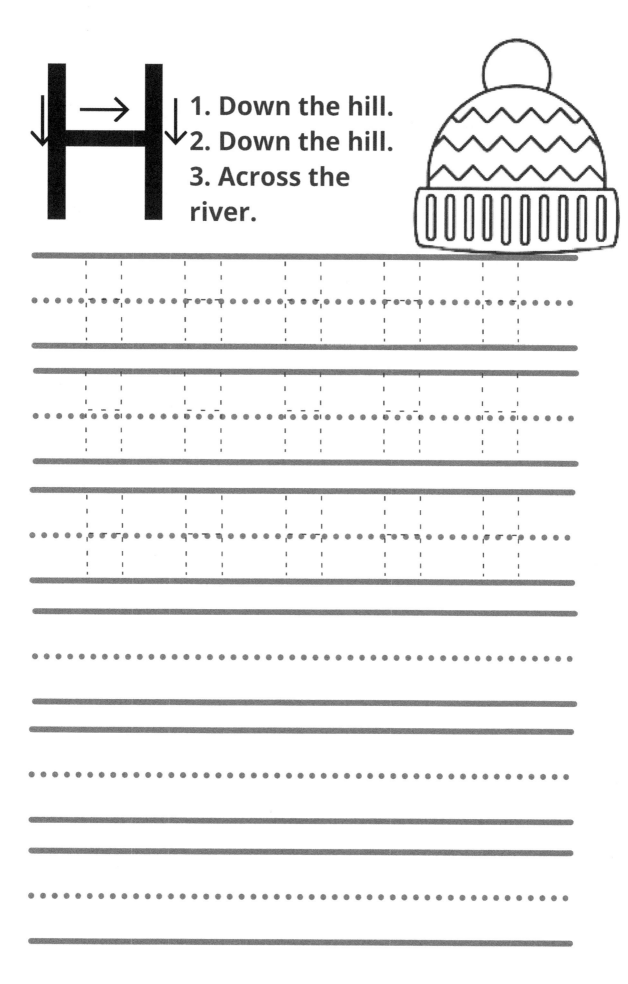

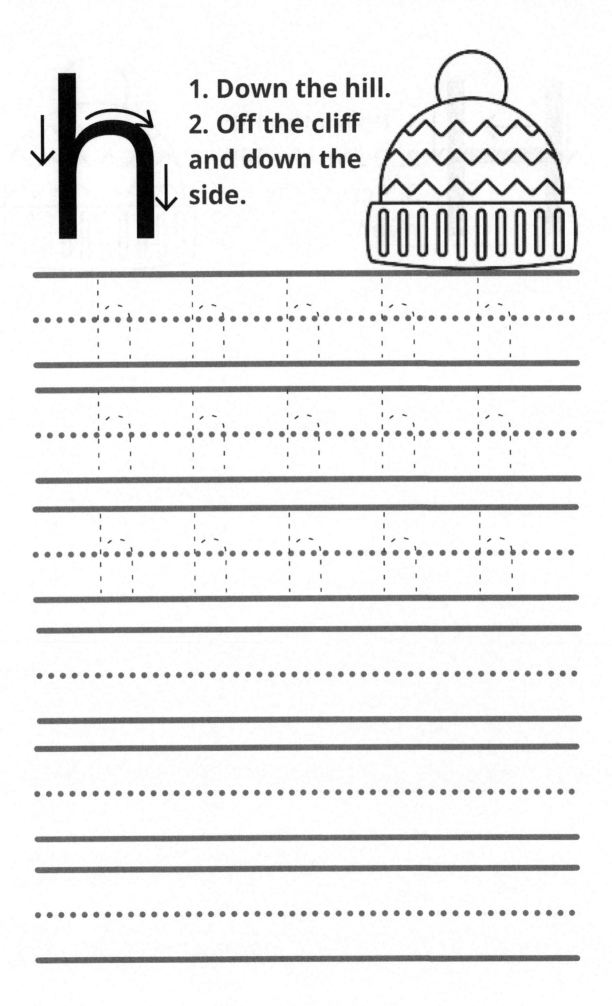

1. Down the hill.
2. Off the cliff and down the side.

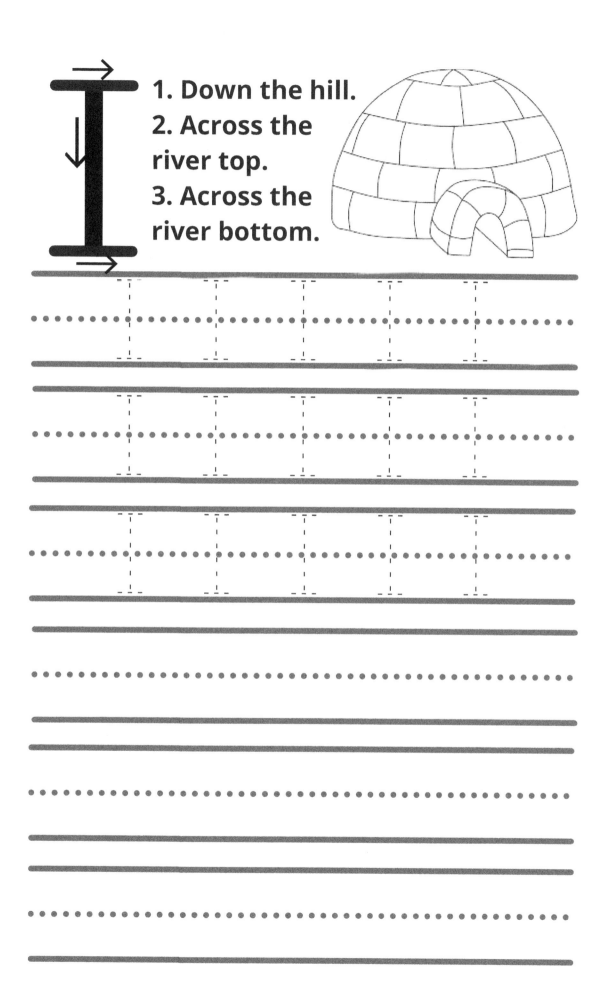

1. Down the hill.
2. Across the river top.
3. Across the river bottom.

1. Down the hill.
2. Make a dot.

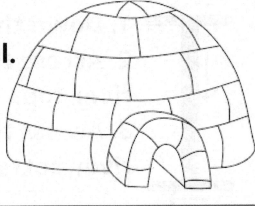

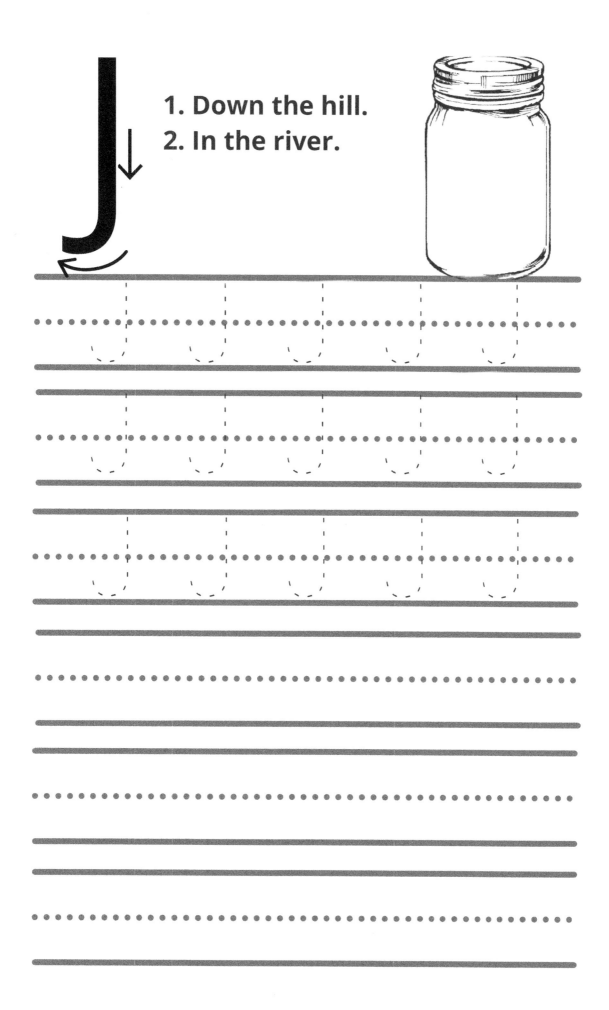

1. Down the hill.
2. In the river.

j
1. Down the hill.
2. In the river.
3. Make a dot.

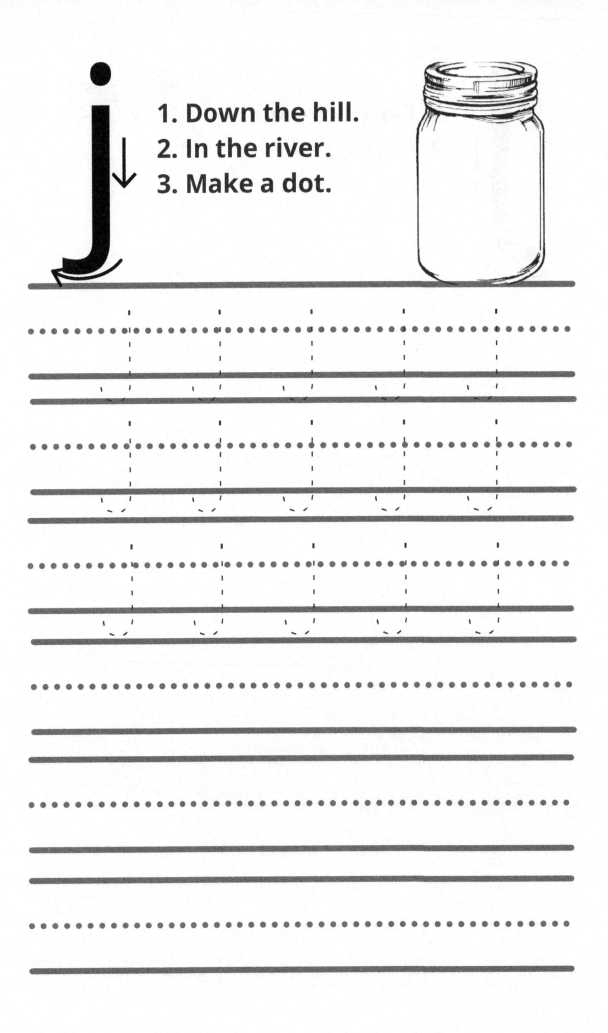

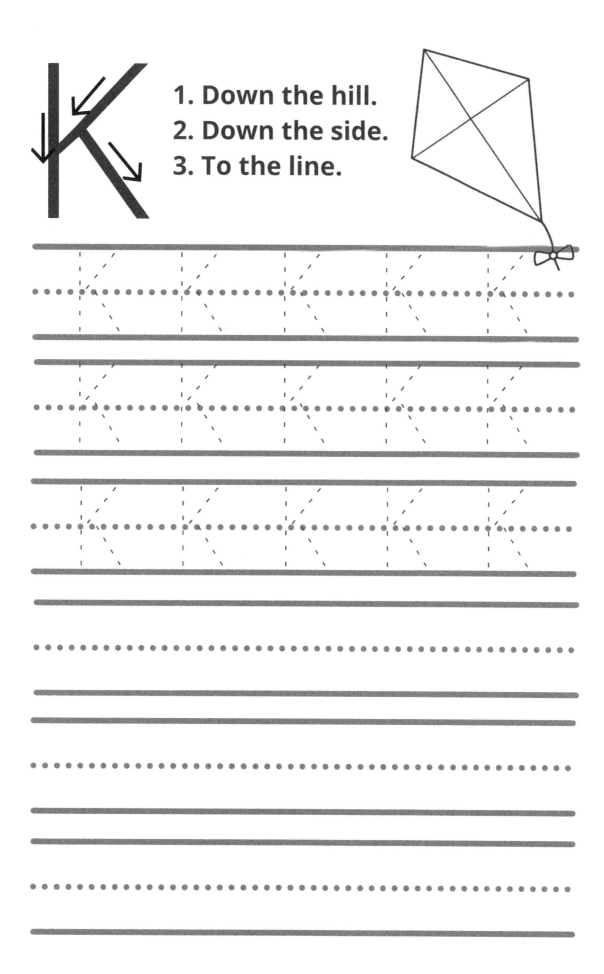

1. Down the hill.
2. Down the side.
3. To the line.

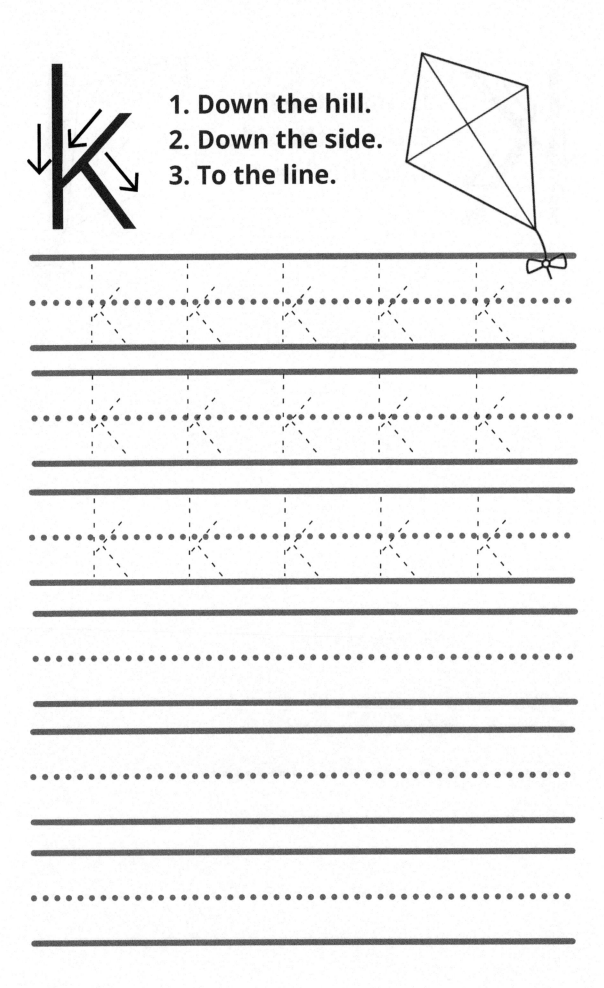

1. Down the hill.
2. Along the line.

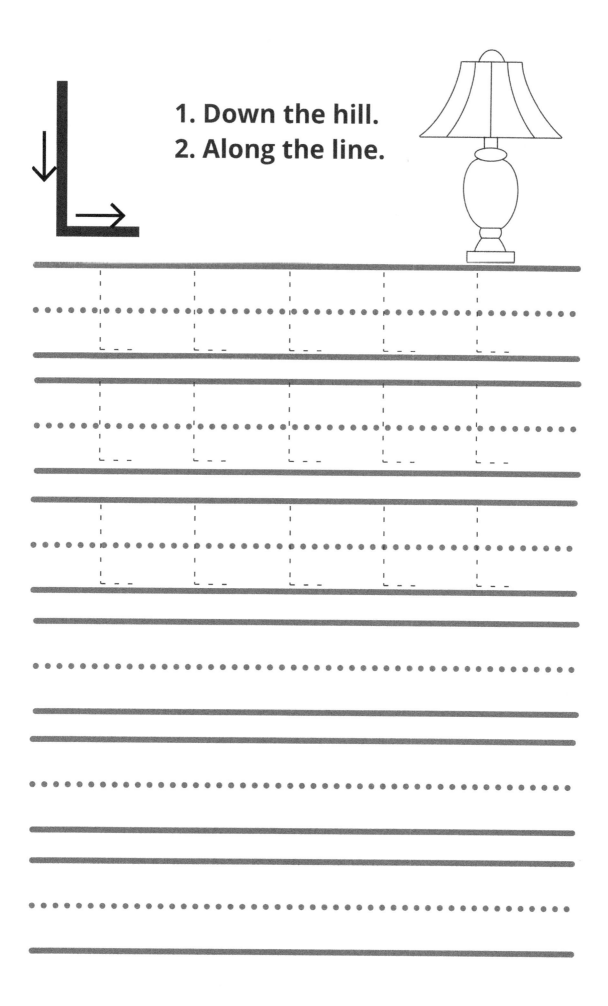

1. Down the hill.

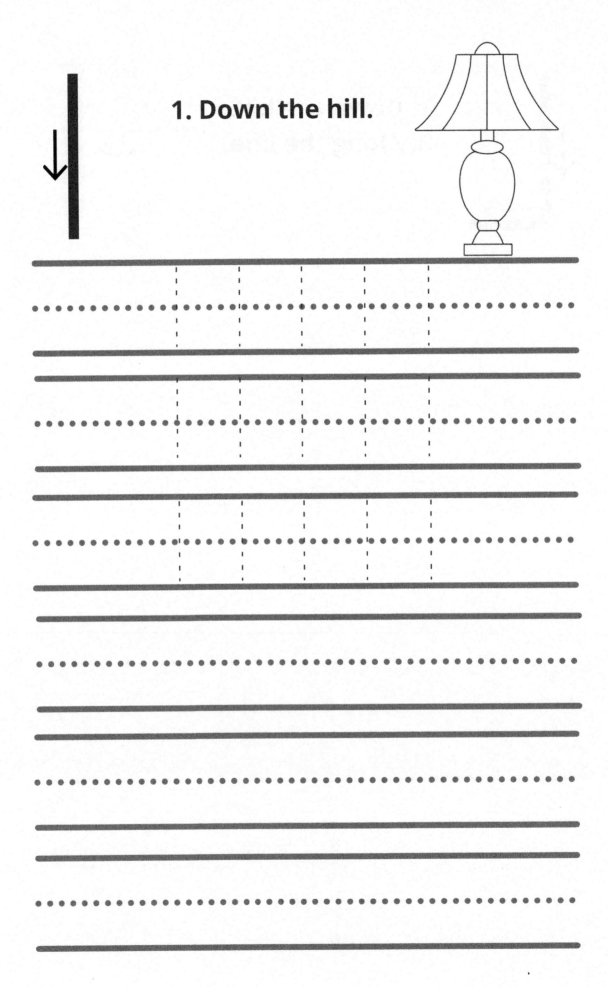

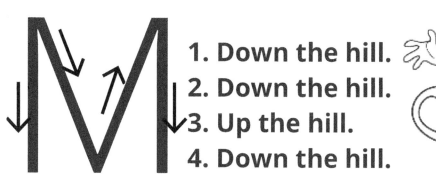

1. Down the hill.
2. Down the hill.
3. Up the hill.
4. Down the hill.

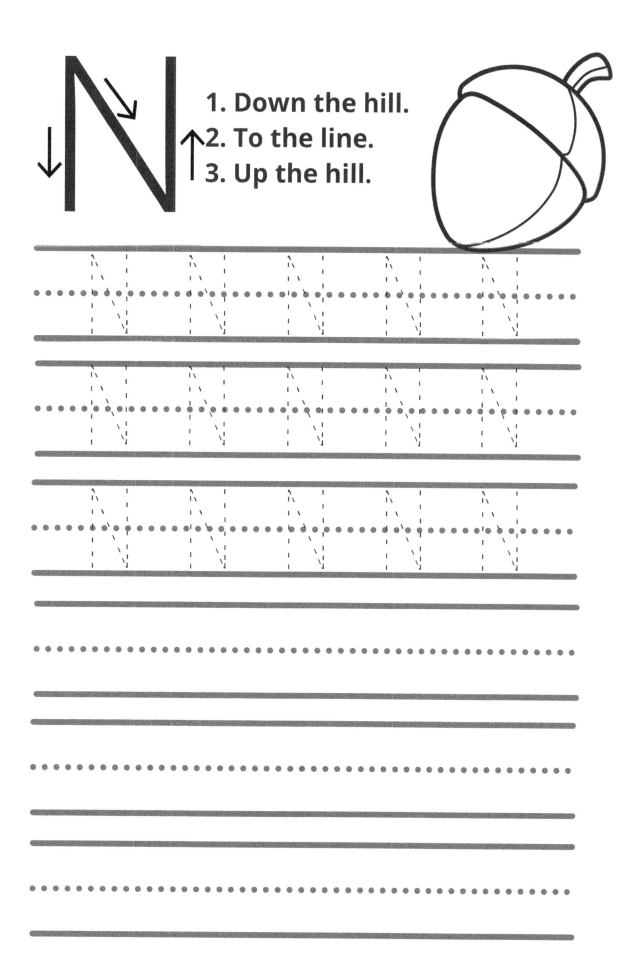

1. Down the hill.
2. To the line.
3. Up the hill.

1. Down the hill.
2. Over the mountain.

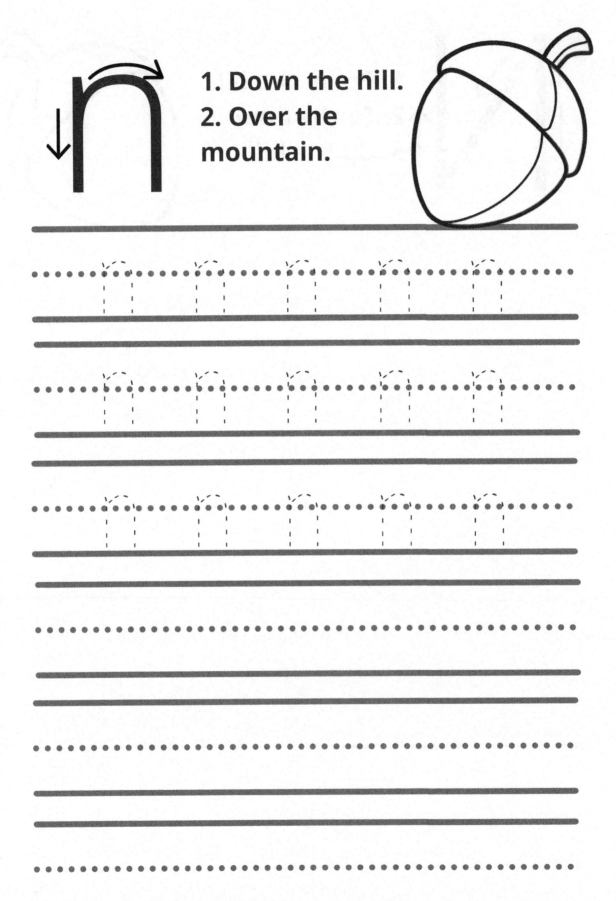

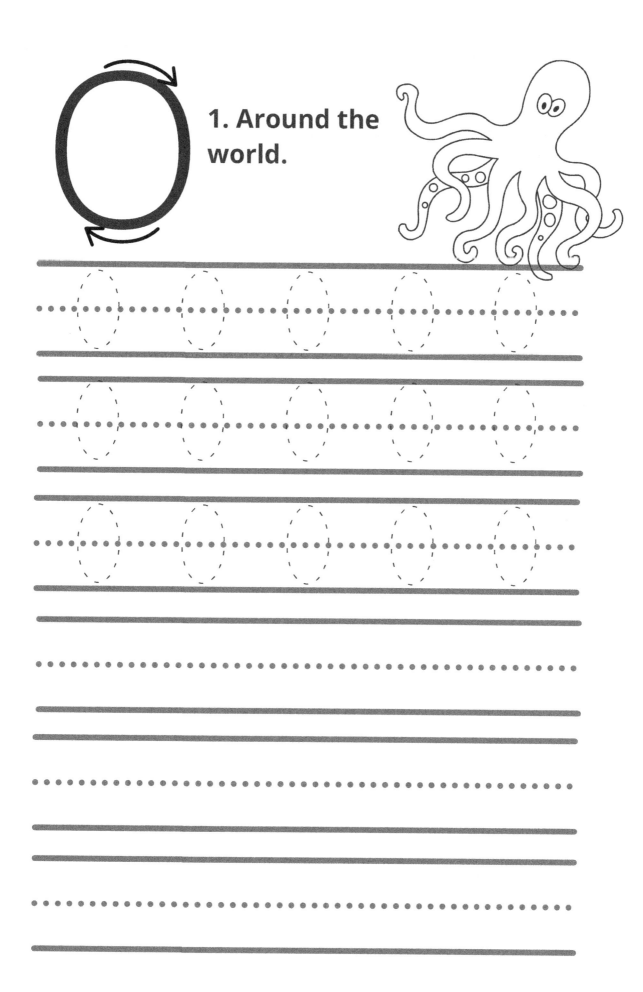

1. Around the world.

 1. Around the world.

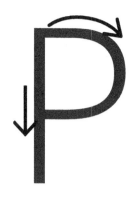

1. Down the hill.
2. Around the world.

1. Down the hill (below the line.)
2. Around the world.

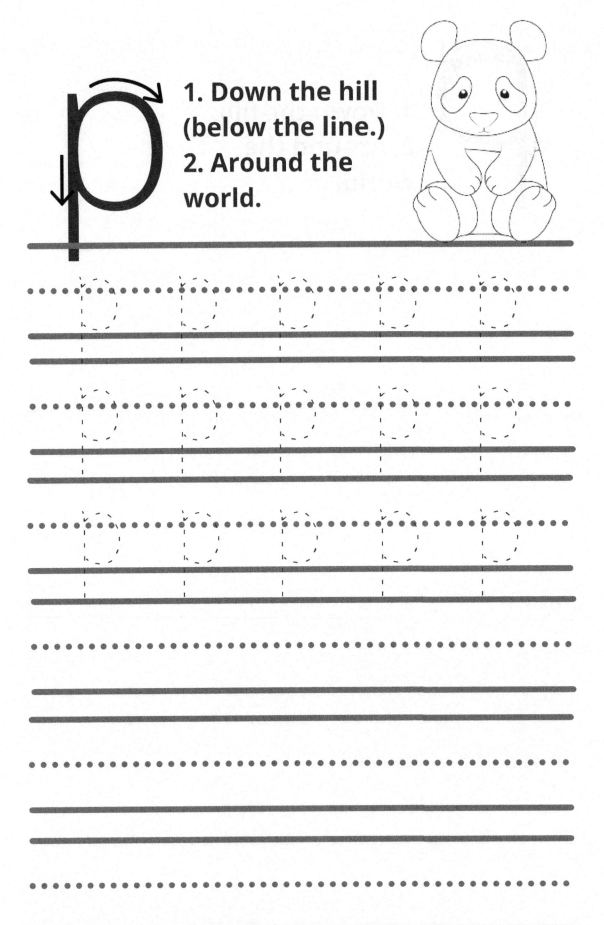

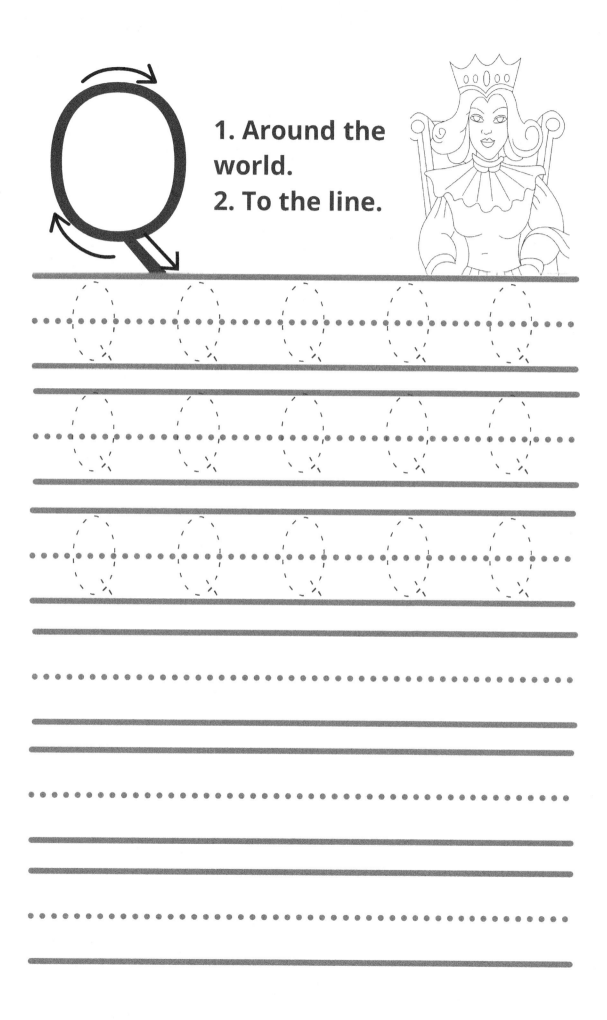

1. Around the world.
2. To the line.

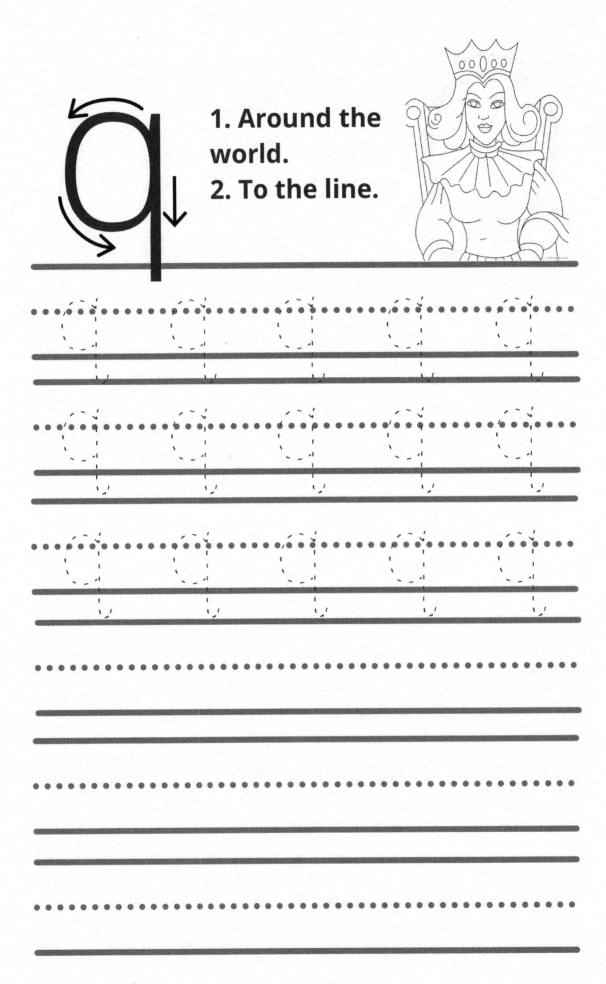

1. Around the world.
2. To the line.

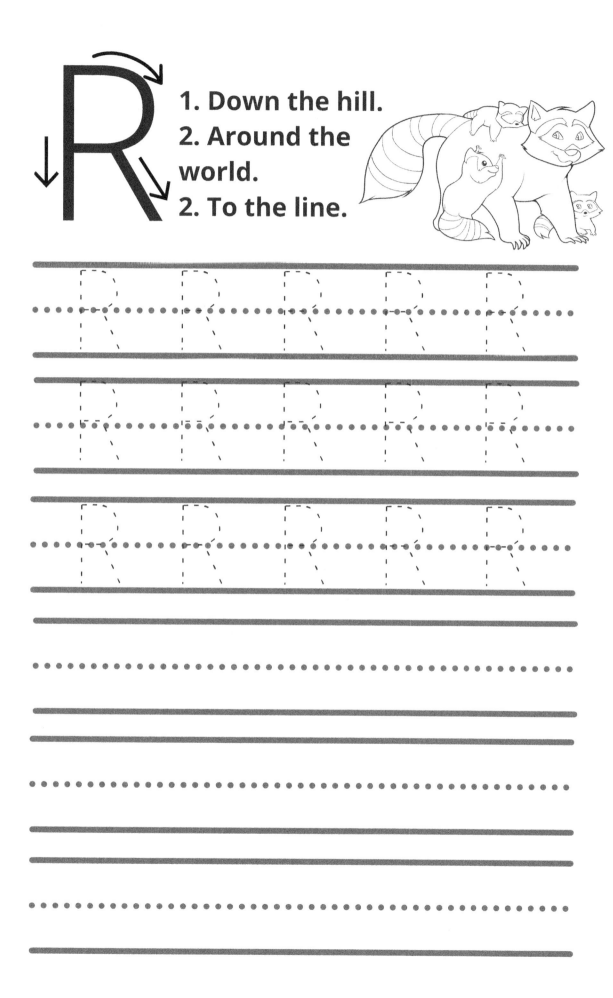

1. Down the hill.
2. Half way over the mountain.

1. Curve back.
2. Curve down.
3. Curve back.

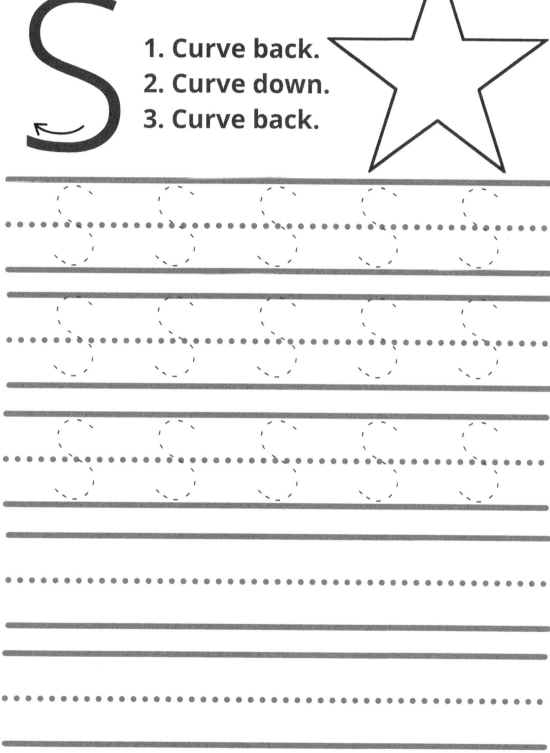

1. Curve back.
2. Curve down.
3. Curve back.

1. Down the hill.
2. Across the top.

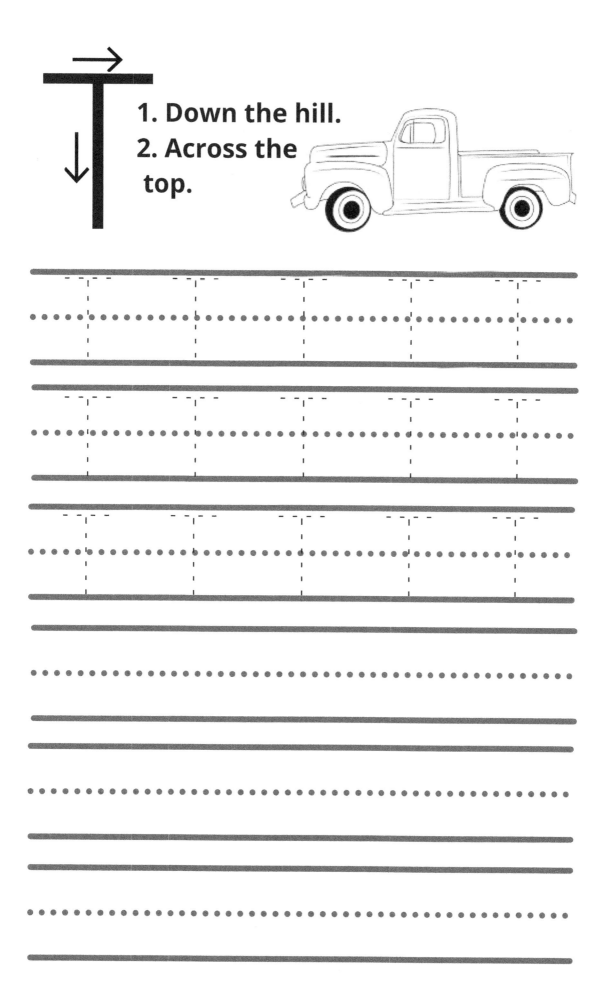

1. Down the hill.
2. Across the middle.

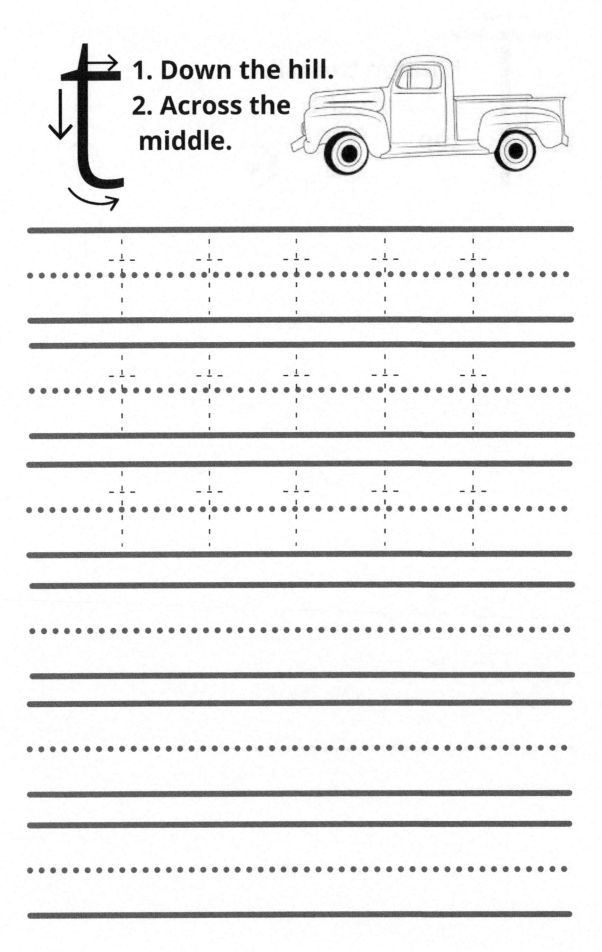

1. Down the hill.
2. Come straight up the mountain.

1. Down the hill.
2. Come straight up the mountain.

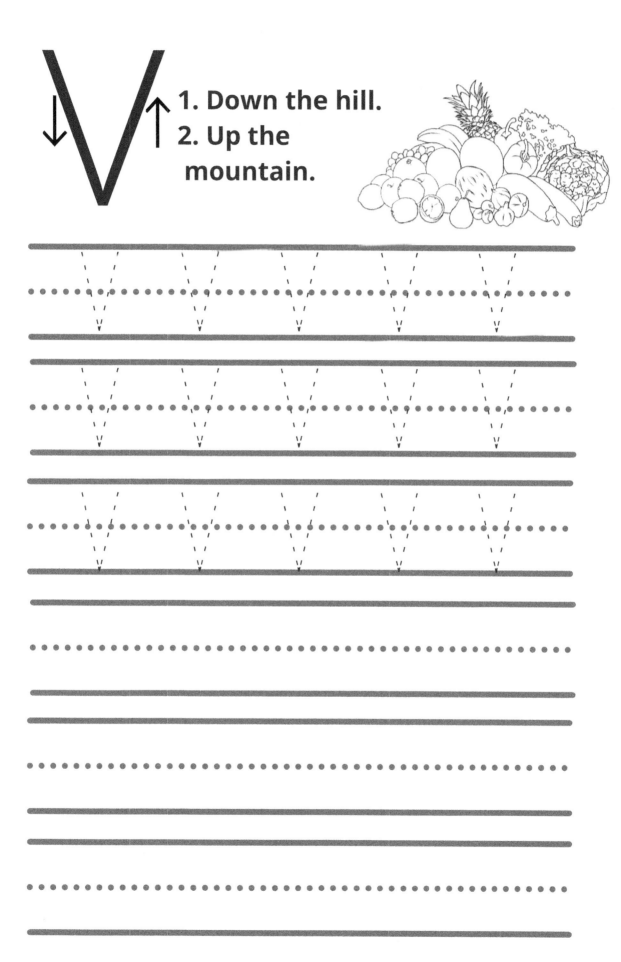

1. Down the hill.
2. Up the mountain.

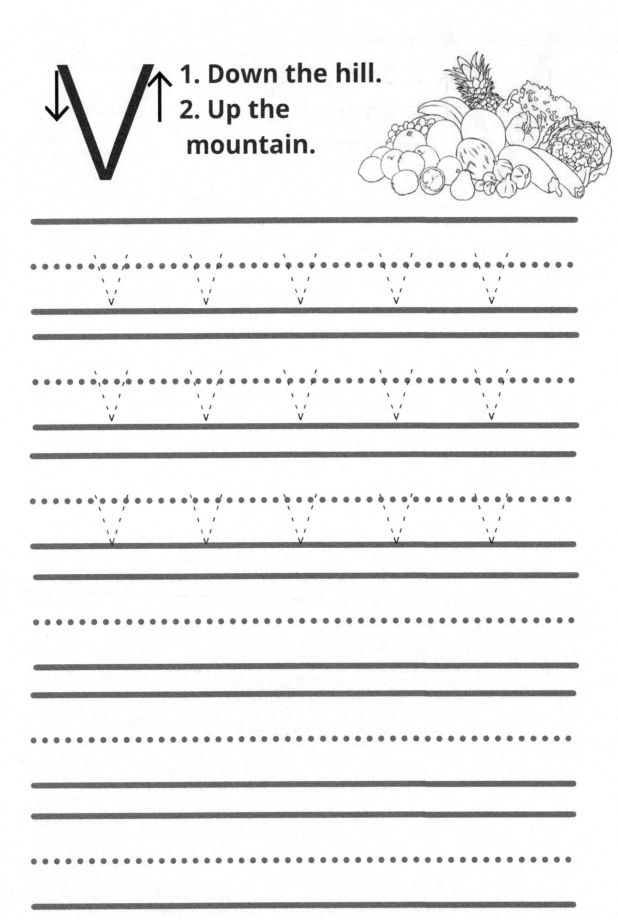

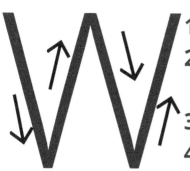

1. Down the hill.
2. Up the mountain.
3. Down the hill.
4. Up the mountain.

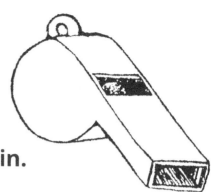

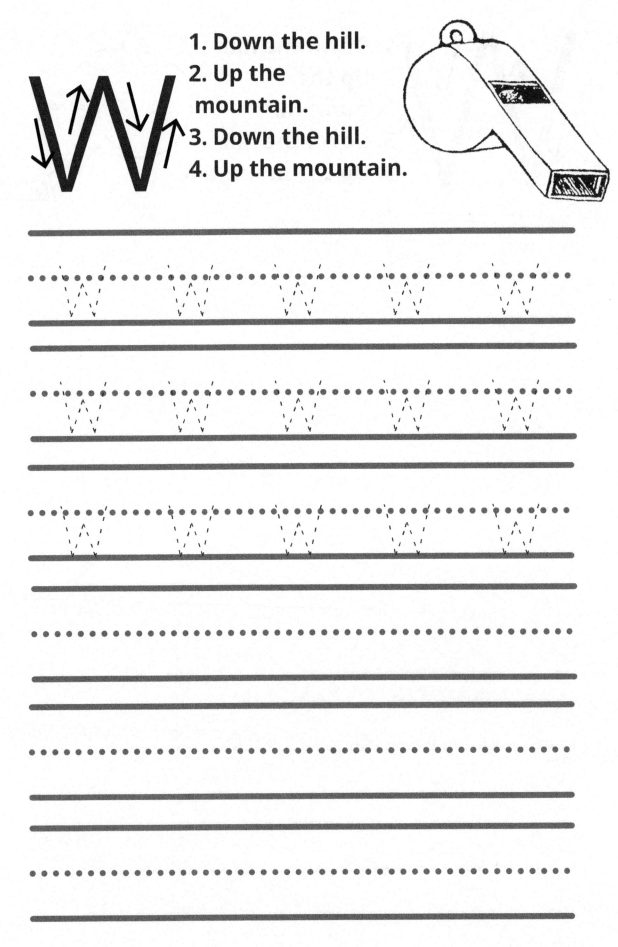

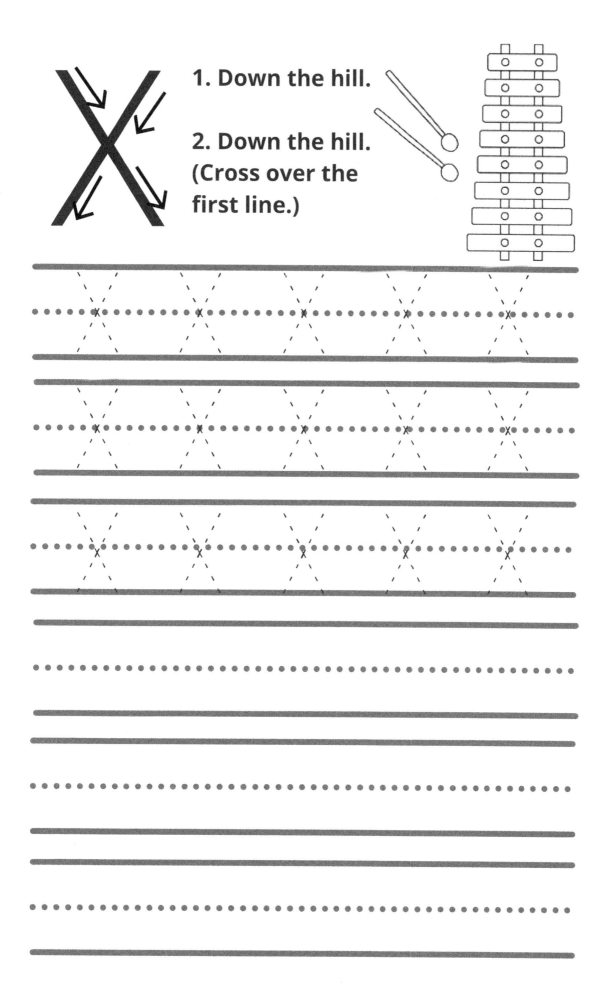

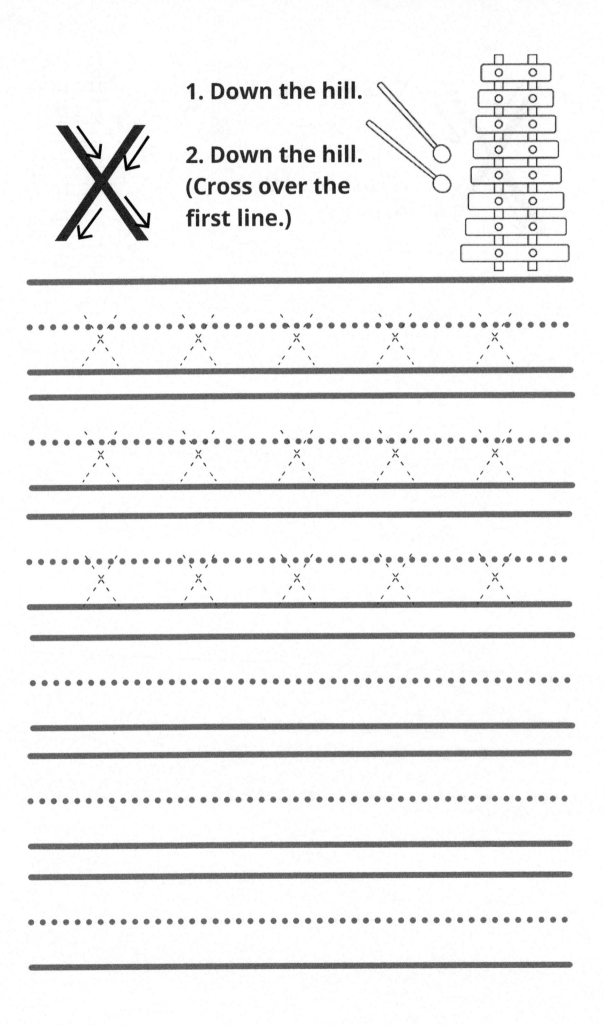

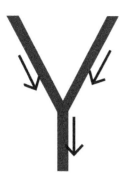

1. Down the hill.
2. Down the hill. (Form a V)
3. Down the hill sit on the line.

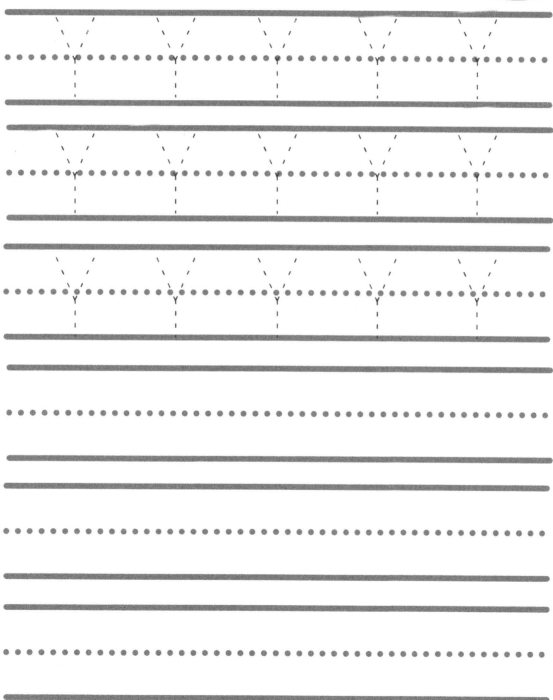

1. Down the hill.
2. Down the hill. (Form a V)
3. Down the hill sit below the line.

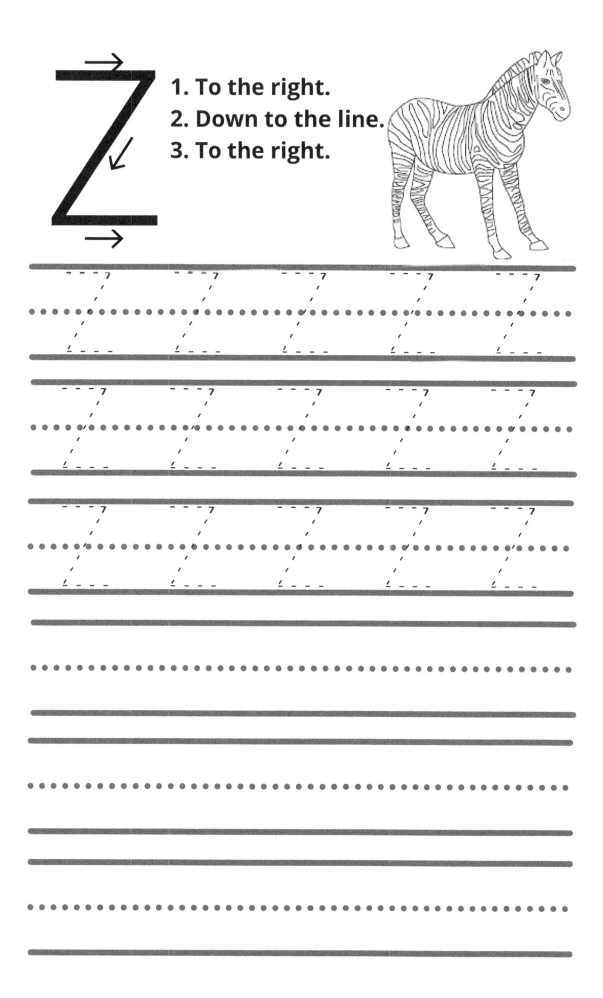

1. To the right.
2. Down to the line.
3. To the right.

1. To the right.
2. Down to the line.
3. To the right.

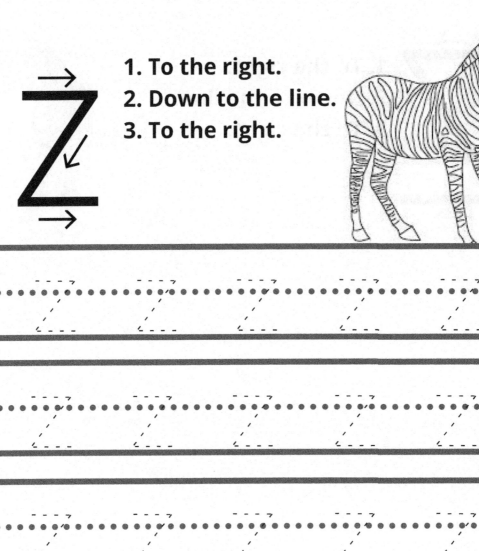

Made in the USA
Columbia, SC
24 August 2022